THE WILD HUNT

CHILDREN'S NORSE FOLKTALES

Speedy Publishing LLC
40 E. Main St. #1156
Newark, DE 19711
www.speedypublishing.com

The myth of the Wild Hunt is sometimes told this way:

- When the winds in winter blow and the fires of Yule are lit, you had better stay indoors and shut yourself safely away from dark paths and the wild heath.

People wandering outside, all by themselves, on these Yule nights could hear a sudden rustling thru the treetops – rustling that could be the wind, even though everything in the wood seems still.

Then the loud barking of dogs could fill the air, and the wild souls sweep down, and the black hounds' eyes flash with fire.

Woden was regarded as the leader of disembodied spirits – the gatherer of those who have died. The dead souls were wafted on the winds of a storm.

Woden's passing is accompanied by strangely furious winds, thunder, and lightning.

Through the years, the myth has been adapted to suit the time period and the geography of the area where it is told.

For example, in the Middle Ages, kings and leaders like Charlemagne, King Arthur, and Frederick Barbarossa loved to hunt, so the storm of spirits is like a ghostly hunting party.

Another folktale stated later that Hans von Hackelnberg could be the leader. He was believed to have slain a boar but was injured and died of poison.

He declared that he did not wish to go to heaven, but wanted to hunt forever.

The wish was granted and he was given permission, or maybe cursed, so he could hunt in the night sky.

Still another version stated that this was his punishment. Either way, in these versions he was the leader of the Wild Hunt.

How was the myth interpreted?

This is a folk myth of the European people about some supernatural ghostly huntsmen who were wildly pursuing, or hunting something.

The hunters are believed to be spirits of dead people, fairies, or elves. Their leader was often named as Woden or Odin.

The Wild Hunt was thought to foreshadow catastrophes like war or plague, or death to the one who witnesses the event.

Others also believed that people who encountered the Hunt could be abducted into the fairy kingdom or to the underworld. Some believed that the spirits of people who are asleep could be pulled to join the ghostly ride.

CONCLUSION

In this myth, the Wild Hunt, a number of themes connect powerfully to the underworld, and what happens after death.

For the ancient Germans, it was possible to pass between the worlds of the dead and the living during midwinter.

This myth may relate to ancestor-worship or the cult of the dead, who could continue to exist in a plane of being between earth and heaven.

Did you enjoy reading?
Don't forget to share this to
your friends!

www.ingramcontent.com/pod-product-compliance
Lightning Source LLC
LaVergne TN
LVHW060513170826
845677LV00026B/1728
* 9 7 9 8 8 6 9 4 4 4 7 3 8 *